2487

D1716417

Sir Frederick Banting

Doctor Against Diabetes

Sir Frederick
Banting
Doctor
Against
Diabetes

by Ann Margaret Mayer
illustrated by Harold Henriksen

Creative Education
Mankato, Minnesota 56001

Published by Creative Education, 123 South Broad Street,
P. O. Box 227, Mankato, Minnesota 56001
Text copyright © 1974 by Ann Mayer. Illustrations copyright © 1974 by Creative
Education. No part of this book may be reproduced in any form without written
permission from the publisher. International copyrights reserved in all
countries. Printed in the United States.
Distributed by Childrens Press, 1224 West Van Buren Street, Chicago, Illinois 60607
Library of Congress Numbers: 74-2048   ISBN: 0-87191-323-2

Library of Congress Cataloging in Publication Data
Mayer, Ann Margaret, 1938-
Sir Frederick Banting, doctor against diabetes.
(Personal close ups)
SUMMARY: Recounts the life of the Canadian doctor who discovered the
means of keeping the once fatal disease of diabetes under control.
1. Banting, Sir Frederick Grant, 1891-1941–Juvenile literature.
[1. Banting, Sir Frederick Grant, 1891-1941. 2. Physicians. 3. Diabetes]
I. Henriksen, Harold, illus. II. Title.
R464.B3M38   616.4'62'00924 [B] [92]   74-2048   ISBN 0-87191-323-2

INTRODUCTION

About 4 million people in the United States suffer from a disease called diabetes. This is not a contagious disease. It occurs when something goes wrong with an organ of the body called the pancreas.

The pancreas has two important jobs. One of them is to make a substance called insulin. Our bodies need insulin in order to change the food we eat into energy. Most of our energy comes from foods containing sugar and starch.

A diabetic person does not have enough insulin. His body is unable to burn sugar and change it into energy. Large amounts of sugar build up in his blood. Although he eats plenty, he grows thin and weak. He may fall into a deep sleep, called a coma. Unless he receives insulin, he will not be able to live long.

Dr. Frederick Banting was the man who discovered insulin. Before Dr. Bantings' discovery, diabetics could expect to live only a few years. Today they are able to live normal, healthy lives. Dr. Banting is one of the world's greatest medical heroes.

Sir Frederick

Banting
Doctor
Against
Diabetes

It was a cold Canadian winter evening in 1902. The river near the Banting's farm in Alliston was crowded with skaters. Some children stood warming themselves beside a bonfire on the ice.

Eleven-year-old Fred Banting and his sister Esther were gathering wood for the fire. Suddenly they heard some sharp barks. Glancing up they saw their pet collie dashing toward them. Collie looked at Fred and whined. Then he trotted a few steps toward the house, turning to see if the children were following.

"Collie acts like there's something wrong, Esther," said Fred. "We'd better go home and see."

Quickly they shouldered their skates and hurried up the hill. Collie bounded ahead toward the red brick farmhouse. As they opened the kitchen door, they saw Father on the floor. He was groaning and rubbing his legs.

"Papa, what happened?" cried Esther.

"Oh, I'm so glad you're home!" he exclaimed with relief. "I suddenly got cramps in my legs. I fell and couldn't get up by myself."

Fred and Esther helped him into a chair. Then they made him comfortable with a footstool and a blanket.

"You know, Pa," said Fred, "Collie's a smart dog. He's really the one who rescued you. I think he knew Mama was out for the evening, so he came to get us."

There was something special about Collie. He looked out for the farm and every member of the Banting family. Perhaps because Fred was the youngest, Collie took particular care of him. He went everywhere with Fred.

Like every farm boy, Fred had his share of chores to do. Since he had older brothers, he was seldom asked to help with the plowing or planting. Instead he helped care for the horses, cows and pigs.

Mr. Banting was proud of his fine herd of beef cattle. Fred was eager to learn all about the animals. He spent a lot of time in the barn watching his father and asking questions.

When Fred went to the barn, Collie was always at his heels. At night the dog slept in a cozy house under the cherry tree. It had a little porch where Collie could lie in hot weather. When winter came Fred lined the inside with a furry buffalo robe.

On school days Collie was very lonesome. He would follow Fred to the gate and sit down to watch until the boy disappeared over the wooden bridge. In the afternoon Collie was always waiting for Fred in the same spot.

One afternoon on his way home Fred stopped to watch some workmen building a house. They were standing on a platform high above the ground. All of a sudden, he heard a loud crack. Before he knew what had happened, the men came plunging down.

Terrified, Fred ran to find the doctor. When he returned a large crowd had gathered. They were relieved to see help arrive. Fred watched with fascination as the doctor examined the men. How skillfully he probed for broken bones and bandaged their cuts! In a short time the doctor was ready to drive the men home in his carriage.

As Fred walked home he kept thinking about what he had seen. "Wouldn't it be wonderful to be able to help people like that!" he thought. From that day on Fred's goal was to become a doctor.

Fred studied hard at school and kept his teachers busy answering his questions. He was never content to memorize things he did not understand.

But Fred didn't·spend all his time studying. He was a star member of the school soccer and baseball teams. He enjoyed sketching and whittling things out of wood. He and his two best friends, Jane and cousin Fred Hipwell, went exploring together for Indian relics. The Bantings' farm had once been the site of a Huron Indian camp. Sometimes the children found arrowheads or pieces of Indian pottery.

Jane enjoyed doing the same things the boys did. She was a strong swimmer and could out-distance both of them in a race. Besides that she could ride horseback and play baseball as well as any boy. Jane got good marks in school, too. She often helped Fred and his cousin with their homework.

Both boys wanted to be doctors. But they knew their fathers hoped they would be ministers. To keep from disappointing them, the cousins thought of a compromise. "We'll be medical missionaries," they decided.

Religion had an important place in the Bantings' life. Mr. and Mrs. Banting were active members of the Methodist church. They saw that the children attended church and Sunday school regularly. Every day began with family prayers and Bible reading.

Fred felt a warm admiration for his parents. Although they were strict, they provided a happy, secure home for their five children. Evenings at home were often more fun than going to parties or dances. Sometimes the family gathered around the organ in the parlor. Mama played while the others sang. Then Papa might read a story aloud.

When Fred was fourteen something happened which

no one could explain to him. Jane, who had been so strong and healthy, suddenly began to lose weight. She no longer felt like playing outside. She had so little energy that she had to drop out of school. The doctor said that she had diabetes.

Fred often went to visit her. He felt frightened to see her growing thinner and thinner. "Won't she ever get well again, Ma?" he asked. Fred wished desperately there was some way he could help her.

"I'm afraid not," Mrs. Banting said sadly. "Doctors don't know any way to cure diabetes."

It was a dreadful blow for Fred when Jane died a few months later. For days he didn't feel like doing anything or talking to anyone.

One evening Papa sat down beside Fred. He laid a hand on Fred's knee. "I know how you've been feeling these last few days, son." His voice was gentle. "Maybe it would help if we talk about it."

"Why did Jane have to die, Pa?" Fred felt the words choking in his throat. "Couldn't anyone help her?"

"Sometimes we must accept things we don't understand, Fred," replied his father. "Perhaps someday doctors will know how to cure diabetes."

Fred was silent for awhile. Suddenly his feeling of helplessness turned into determination. "When I'm a doctor, I'm going to help search for a cure," he resolved.

In the fall of 1910 Fred Banting and Fred Hipwell

entered the University of Toronto. They began their studies to prepare for the ministry.

The city of Toronto was an exciting place for two boys from the country. Fred Banting joined the College Glee Club and made many new friends. Some of the fellows he met were medical students. As they talked about their courses, Fred listened with envy. He had a growing feeling that he had made a mistake in choosing the ministry.

By the spring of his second year, Fred realized the ministry was not for him. His longing to be a doctor made him feel restless and unhappy. Fred Hipwell felt the same way.

Both boys went home to break the news to their parents. Mr. Banting's face reflected his disappointment. But he was understanding. "Fred," he said, "I know you wouldn't change your mind without careful thought. I can see your interest really lies in medicine."

That fall Fred and his cousin returned to Toronto University as medical students. This time Fred threw himself into his studies. A whole new world opened before him which absorbed him completely. He spent hours in the laboratory preparing slides and doing experiments.

During his second year Fred saved enough money to buy his own microscope. Sometimes he became so interested in his work that he forgot to eat. In many of his courses he did far more than the professor asked.

Although Fred's grades were mostly C's he was a careful,

diligent worker. Sometimes the other students kidded him for spending so much time studying. However, Fred was popular with his classmates. He had a direct, friendly manner and a good sense of humor.

Throughout his years in college, Fred continued to take part in sports. He joined the Rugby football team. His success as an athlete was much greater than his success as a scholar.

Fred had been in medical school only two years when World War I broke out. Many young men began to enlist in the Canadian Armed Forces. Fred wanted to join the infantry immediately.

Most of the professors urged the medical students to complete their courses first. "You will be much more valuable to your country as doctors," they said.

So Fred stayed in school. On December 4, 1916, he earned his medical degree. The next day he joined the Canadian Army Medical Corps. After a short training period he was sent overseas.

Banting was first assigned to a hospital in England. There he learned bone surgery from a skillful surgeon, Dr. Clarence Starr. By the time his training ended, Banting had decided he wanted to be a surgeon.

Banting's next assignment put him on the front line of battle. As a member of the Field Ambulance Corps, he was sent to Cambrai, France. This area was the scene of some of the fiercest fighting in the war.

Banting was in charge of a first aid post a short distance

from the trenches. Guns were booming all around him. Wounded men were carried in faster then he and his partners could handle them. Banting worked tirelessly washing cuts, setting bones and bandaging wounds.

During a brief lull, he went to the doorway to look out. At that instant a shell exploded a few feet away. A fragment of the shell flew through the air, hitting Banting's right arm.

Major Palmer, who was working with Banting, examined his arm immediately. "This is serious, Fred," he said. "It's cut an artery. I'm going to bind your arm and send you to a hospital right away."

"It's not that bad," Banting protested. "I can't leave you here alone to take care of all these men."

Before Palmer could reply, he received orders to report to another first aid station. Banting continued to work for another 17 hours. When Palmer returned he found Banting so weak he could hardly stand. His arm had begun to bleed again. This time Palmer got him into an ambulance.

Back in England in a hospital, Banting began to get restless. His wound was not healing properly. When the surgeon examined it he looked worried.

"Your wound is infected," he told Banting. "The infection is likely to spread unless I amputate part of your arm."

"Lose my right arm!" Banting refused to consider such a thing. He knew that this would end his dream of becoming a surgeon.

"I'm going to keep my arm," he declared. Being a

doctor, he knew the risk he was taking. He decided to supervise the care of the arm himself.

As the months dragged by, Banting's arm began to heal. Then he received some surprising and unexpected news. The British Government had awarded him the Military Cross for his bravery in France. This award had a special meaning for Banting. It reminded him how grateful he was to still have his arm.

At last the war ended and Banting returned to Toronto. Here he spent the next year at the Hospital for Sick Children. Banting worked closely with the skilled Dr. Starr learning how to perform bone surgery on children.

Many of his patients were crippled children. Banting loved children and found great satisfaction in helping them. They looked forward to his daily visits to the wards. He delighted them with stories, jokes and funny nicknames.

After a year at the hospital, Banting was ready to set up his own practice. He moved to the city of London in western Ontario. Here he thought he would have plenty of patients.

Banting bought a house on a pleasant, shady street. To furnish his office he had to borrow money from his brother. However, he was certain he could repay it quickly.

A few days later he hung out his shingle and sat down to wait for patients. At the end of a week not a single one had come. Banting sat at his desk reading medical books and journals to pass the time. Two weeks went by and then three.

When the first month had passed and still no patients appeared, Banting felt discouraged. Doubts arose in his mind. "Perhaps I shouldn't have become a doctor," he thought.

To fill his empty days, Banting took up painting. Time dragged on and things got no better. At the end of three months Banting had earned only $12. This wasn't even enough to buy his food! He knew he could not sit around and wait any longer.

There was a medical school in London, so Banting applied for a teaching position. He was given two courses to teach. Along with teaching he was asked to assist another doctor with laboratory work. This was his first taste of research. What he learned from Dr. Miller later proved very valuable.

One day Banting was preparing a lecture on the pancreas. As he read about this organ he realized how little scientists knew about it. They knew that the pancreas made a juice which aided digestion. They also knew that if the pancreas was removed from an animal, it became diabetic.

Once more Banting began to think about diabetes. What could he tell his students about this disease? They would be sure to ask him questions he couldn't answer. He went to the library to find out more about it. Among the articles he read, one especially caught his attention. It described some experiments which an American doctor had done

on the pancreas.

Well past midnight Banting suddenly got an idea. He grabbed a notebook and jotted down a plan for a new experiment. No one had yet proved that the pancreas made something which prevented diabetes. But scientists had observed a special group of cells which appeared to produce such a substance.

"I think I know a way to remove this substance from these cells," he thought excitedly.

Banting didn't sleep a wink that night. He could hardly wait until morning to talk over his plan with Dr. Miller.

When Dr. Miller heard Banting's idea, he was eager to see it carried out. "I wish I could offer you my laboratory," he said. "But I don't have the equipment you'd need. You must go talk to Dr. Macleod at the University of Toronto. He's an expert on diabetes research."

Two weeks later Banting was on his way to Toronto. As he jolted along in his old Ford, he began to feel nervous. Dr. Macleod was a brilliant man. He had taught for fifteen years, done important research and written scientific articles. Would such a man pay attention to an unsuccessful, twenty-nine-year-old doctor?

As Banting had feared, Macleod barely listened to his ideas. "What makes you think you can succeed where others have failed?" he asked. His voice sounded scornful. "You don't have the training or background to carry out this kind of research."

Banting left Macleod's office feeling very discouraged. But he was not ready to give up. "I don't think I explained my experiment clearly," he thought. "I'll go back tomorrow and try again."

Macleod was clearly annoyed to see this young doctor return. This time Banting asked if he might use Macleod's laboratory while he was on vacation. Rather unwillingly, Macleod agreed. He also promised to find Banting an assistant and provide ten dogs. "But I can't pay either of you," he warned. Banting's spirits were already beginning to rise. Somehow he would scrape together enough money for the summer.

In May 1921 Banting piled all his belongings into his rickety Ford. He had sold his house and given up his teaching job. From here on, his future rested on the success of his experiment.

When Banting met his assistant, he knew right away they would make a good team. Charles Best was one of Macleod's students. Although he was only twenty-one, he had a brilliant record and was an expert chemist. Furthermore he had a special interest in diabetes. His favorite aunt had died from this disease the year before.

There were several steps in Banting's experiment. First he would operate on the pancreas of several dogs. Then he would wait six weeks, open them up and remove the pancreas. Perhaps he could then obtain from it the substance which acted on diabetes.

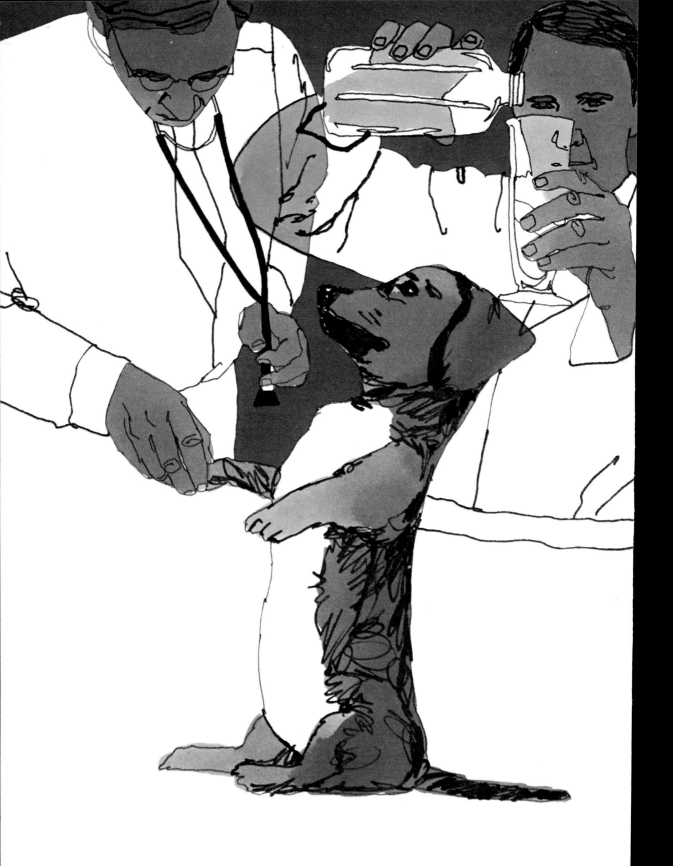

When the first operations were finished, Banting and Best began their wait. They filled in the time swapping war stories, singing and taking care of the dogs.

All of the dogs became their personal friends. Banting treated them like pets. Instead of keeping them in cages, he let them run freely around the lab. Soon they trusted him completely. They even allowed him to take blood samples from their paws while they were awake.

Banting knew that he would have to sacrifice some of these dogs. This made him sad. But he thought of the dogs as brave soldiers. They were giving their lives in a battle against disease. Someday this might make it possible to save thousands of human lives.

When the weeks of waiting were over, Banting operated again. But to his dismay, something had gone wrong with the first operations. The pancreas was not ready to be removed.

Time was pressing. Macleod would return in two weeks. Banting could not afford to wait much longer. He operated carefully.

Then bad luck set in. Several dogs died. The men had no money to buy more, so Banting sold his car. But they had one lucky break. Macleod did not return as early as they had expected.

After two weeks Banting examined each dog's pancreas. Yes, now he could remove it! Both men rushed into action. Banting finished operating and sewed the first dog up carefully. Best prepared test tubes and beakers of chemicals. Then he took the pancreas, ground it up and prepared a fluid.

Soon the most important moment in the experiment was at hand. They were ready to test the substance which they had prepared. What would happen when they injected it into a diabetic dog?

An appealing yellow and white dog lay limp and panting on the table. Her pancreas had been removed. Now she was in a diabetic coma. At the most she had only a few hours to live. Best took a sample of her blood. It was filled with sugar — a sign of severe diabetes. Then Banting prepared the injection.

Both men were hopeful, yet fearful. They paced the room and waited in silence. In half an hour Best tested the dog's blood. There was no change. After another half hour, he tested it again. Banting did not need to wait for Best to tell him that a miracle was happening. He could already see signs that the dog was recovering. It opened its eyes, raised its head and whined. With joy and excitement, Best exclaimed, "The sugar in her blood has dropped!"

Scarcely daring to believe what they saw, the two men stared at the dog. After awhile it sat up. Best continued to take blood samples every half hour. In a short time the dog was walking around the lab, wagging its tail and begging for food. Tests showed that the amount of sugar in its blood was normal.

"Could it really be true?" they wondered. "Have we discovered a cure for diabetes?"

Yet Banting and Best were not ready to claim complete success. They both knew that this was only the beginning. Many more tests and experiments lay ahead.

This new substance which Banting and Best had discovered was named insulin. Banting soon found that insulin did not cure diabetes. It only kept the disease under control. When the supply of insulin ran out, the diabetic dogs died. It was clear that a large amount of insulin would be needed to keep diabetic people alive. Banting and Best began a search for a better way to obtain it.

In September Macleod returned. He was astonished to read the reports of the experiment. Of course he wanted to see proof of their success.

"I think you're on the right track," he agreed. "But a lot of work remains to be done."

Macleod allowed Banting and Best to continue using his laboratory. But he told them they would have to work alone. "I'm too busy to help you," he said.

After several weeks of searching, Banting found a better source of insulin. He could use the pancreas of cattle after they were butchered for meat.

Now that Banting had larger amounts of insulin, he could test it on human diabetics. Would it work as well on people as it had on dogs?

First Banting and Best had to be sure it was safe to

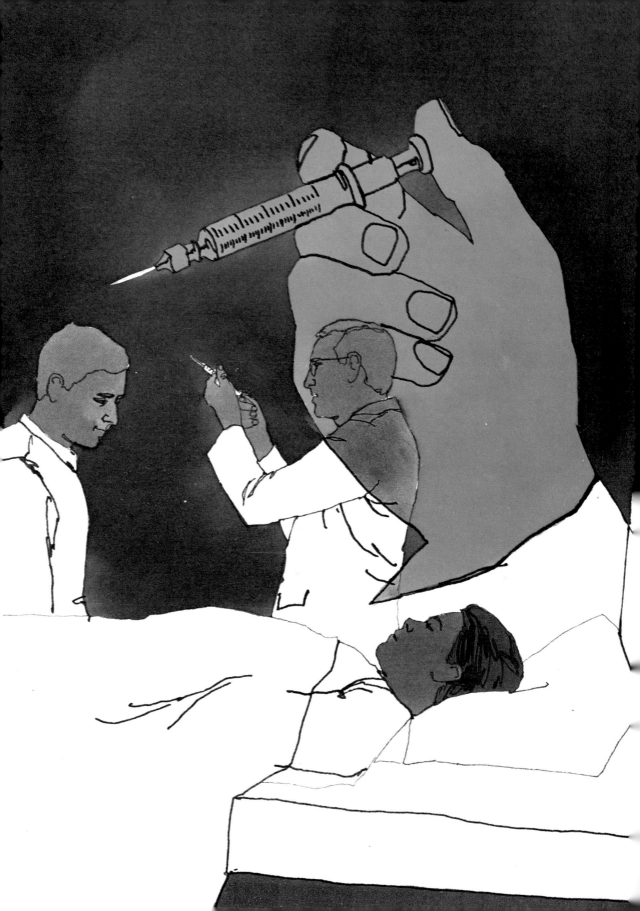

use on humans. They prepared injections to test on themselves. The injections proved harmless. Now they could move on to the most important test.

January 11, 1922 was a great day in medical history. A fourteen-year-old boy with severe diabetes had been admitted to Toronto General Hospital. Doctors had little hope that Leonard Thompson would live. He was as thin as a skeleton and too weak to do anything but lie in bed. Leonard's parents readily agreed to insulin injections.

Changes came more slowly in Leonard than they had in the dogs. Yet there was no doubt that the insulin was working. His energy returned. He no longer felt wildly thirsty and hungry.

Leonard continued to improve daily. A few weeks later he left the hospital. Although he would need insulin every day, Leonard could look forward to a healthy life.

What a great moment this was for Banting! The joy of seeing Leonard recover lessened the painful memory of Jane's death.

Still insulin was not ready to use on large numbers of people. Doctors had a lot to learn about it. What amount did people need? How often should they have it? Was there any danger in giving a diabetic too much insulin?

Banting started giving insulin to diabetics at the Veterans Hospital in Toronto. Nurses and doctors were astonished by the results. Men who had been too ill to move were suddenly restored to health.

In November, 1921 the first public announcement was made about insulin. As word of the discovery spread, Banting became famous almost overnight.

Diabetics, hearing of the miracle of insulin, began flocking to Toronto. They came from all over the world. Some were too sick to walk. Some could speak only a few words of English. Yet all found their way to Banting's doorstep.

Banting had not planned to go into medical practice again. However, many diabetics would see no other doctor. He was too kind to turn anyone away. So he opened an office.

Banting and Best might have made a fortune from insulin. But they believed that medical discoveries belonged to the whole world. They turned over all the profits to the University of Toronto for medical research.

Every day Banting received letters from diabetics thanking him for saving their lives. Letters from children brought him the deepest joy. A number of grateful diabetics came to thank Banting in person. They wanted to see and shake the hand of this great doctor.

All this attention was a strain on Banting. He was a shy, modest man who did not enjoy being in the spotlight. He felt that people were giving him too much glory. He reminded them that Best and several others deserved a large share of the credit.

In the next few years Banting received one honor after

another. He was awarded a gold medal from the University of Toronto. At the age of thirty-two he became the University's first professor of medical research. That same year the Canadian government voted to pay him a yearly sum of $7,500. He immediately used it to pay back the money he owed his family. Banting never became a rich man. He was far too generous. One of his friends said, "You didn't have to pick his pockets. He would freely give you the contents."

The mayor of Alliston gave a public reception in Banting's honor. Mr. and Mrs. Banting sat on the speaker's platform with their son. In his speech Banting gave special thanks to his parents. "Their sacrifices made it possible for me to undertake my research," he said.

Sometime later a reporter asked Mrs. Banting, "Aren't you proud of your son?" She replied modestly, "Not proud, but thankful."

The year 1923 brought Banting the world's highest honor. He and Macleod were chosen to share the Nobel Prize in Medicine. The prize was awarded to them for discovering insulin.

Instead of being pleased, Banting was hurt and angry. "Why wasn't Best included?" he asked. "Surely there must be a mistake. Best was my assistant. He was the one who shared in the discovery."

Outraged that Best had been forgotten, Banting said he would refuse the prize. But Banting's friends would not hear of such a thing.

"The prize is an honor for Canada as well as for you," they said. "You would be hurting your country if you turned it down."

Finally Banting agreed to accept the prize. However, he announced that he would divide his share with Best.

For several years Banting's work had taken up most of his time. He had been to very few parties or social events. As soon as his work became less pressing, he started going out again. He met an attractive young woman named Marion Robertson. In the summer of 1924 they were married.

For the next six years Banting led a quiet life devoted to medical research. Then in 1930 he was appointed director of a new medical research center at the University of Toronto. This center, named the Banting Institute, provided funds for young scientists to do research. Banting had not forgotten his own struggle to get support for his project. Now he was especially interested in helping other young scientists. He turned over his entire share of the Nobel Prize to the Institute.

The job of director was a demanding one. Banting ran the laboratory and advised scientists on their research. At the same time he continued to do research himself.

Banting was a skillful director. He knew how to get people to work well together. Young scientists were never afraid to discuss their ideas with him. He was kind and sympathetic. Above all, he inspired others by his example. Scientists from all over the world came to him for advice.

Although Banting was content with his work, he was not happy at home. He and his wife decided to separate. Banting especially missed his young son, William.

To forget his loneliness he started painting again. One of Canada's leading landscape painters, A. Y. Jackson, became a close friend. Jackson often invited Banting to go with him on sketching trips. They enjoyed adventurous journeys to such remote places as the Eastern Arctic and Northwest Territories.

For the most part Banting's life was quiet. His name even disappeared from the newspapers. However, he had not been forgotten.

In 1934 King George V of England honored him with knighthood. The colorful ceremony took place in Ottawa.

As a knight Banting had a new title. He was Sir Frederick Banting, Knight Commander of the Order of the British Empire. But Banting's title made little difference to him or to those who knew him. At the Institute people fondly called him, "Sir Fred."

In 1938 war again cast its grim shadow on the world. German armies were swallowing up one European country after another. Banting feared another world war was on the way. He spoke to officials in the Canadian government. "Air power will most likely decide the outcome of this war," he said. "We ought to be doing more research in aviation medicine."

The government at once set up a Council of Aviation

Medical Research. Banting was asked to head the council.

On September 1, 1939, Banting enlisted in the army. Nine days later Canada declared war on Germany. Banting soon received his assignment from the government. He was surprised not to be sent to an army hospital. Instead he was asked to direct a program of wartime medical research in Canada and Britain.

Much of his time was spent travelling. He regretted having to leave home, for he was now married again. Banting was making plans to buy a farm in Alliston as soon as the war ended.

Meanwhile the war effort was demanding all his time and energy. Banting directed a study to find out why pilots black out during a power dive. After making these studies, he started to develop a special suit for flyers. It was designed to keep them from blacking out.

In 1941 the suits were ready. Banting had to inform scientists in England about them, so he decided to fly to England himself.

On a cold February day he took a plane from Montreal to Gander, Newfoundland. There he boarded a camouflaged bomber for the flight to England.

It was dusk when the plane took off from Gander. Besides the pilot and radio operator it carried Banting and one other passenger. In a short time the plane left the coast of Newfoundland behind. Ahead lay the Atlantic Ocean, a mantle of black stretching to Europe's distant shores.

Suddenly the plane jerked. Banting heard one of the engines cough. It made another strange sound and then died. The pilot skillfully banked the plane and headed back for Newfoundland. As soon as he sighted land he shouted, "Bail out. I'll bring the plane down."

It was snowing hard. The pilot could not see any landmarks. A huge tree loomed up out of the snowy wasteland. With a crunch the plane clipped the top and crashed into a snow drift.

The pilot was knocked unconscious. He did not know that his passengers had failed to jump out. All three were killed. Three days later rescuers sighted the plane. The pilot was still alive.

When news of Banting's death was made public, people everywhere felt a tremendous sorrow. Diabetics especially felt as if they had lost a close friend.

But the story of Dr. Banting does not end with his death. Research on diabetes still continues.

In 1971 the world celebrated the 50th Anniversary of the discovery of insulin. A special Service of Thanksgiving was held in St. Paul's Cathedral in London. More than 1,200 diabetics attended along with hundreds of others.

Dr. Banting has been honored in many ways — by buildings, by statues, by monuments. But his greatest memorial is not one which has been built by men. It is one which lies in the hearts of those whose lives have been saved by insulin.

Ann Margaret Mayer

Ann Mayer was born in Schenectady, New York and has spent most of her life in upstate New York. She is a graduate of Mount Holyoke College and holds a masters degree in education from Harvard University.

For the past ten years Miss Mayer has been teaching elementary school and is presently teaching third grade in Churchville, New York.

Miss Mayer is the author of a number of short biographical sketches, some for children, which have appeared in periodicals in the United States, Canada and Europe.

Harold Henriksen

Harold was born in St. Paul, Minnesota and has lived there most of his life. He attended the School of the Associated Arts in St. Paul.

Even while serving in the Army, Harold continued to keep alive his desire to become an artist. In 1965 he was a winner in the All Army Art Contest.

After the Army, Harold returned to Minnesota where he worked for several art studios in the Minneapolis-St. Paul area. In 1967 he became an illustrator for one of the largest art studios in Minneapolis.

During 1971 Harold and his wife traveled to South America where he did on-the-spot drawings for a year. Harold, his wife and daughter Maria now live in Minneapolis where he works as a free lance illustrator.

close ups

Walt Disney

Bob Hope

Duke Ellington

Dwight Eisenhower

Coretta King

Pablo Picasso

Ralph Nader

Bill Cosby

Dag Hammarskjold

Sir Frederick Banting

Mark Twain

Beatrix Potter